GREAT CITIES
OF THE WORLD

ISTANBUL

NICOLA BARBER

WORLD ALMANAC® LIBRARY

Please visit our web site at: www.worldalmanaclibrary.com
For a free color catalog describing World Almanac® Library's list of high-quality books
and multimedia programs, call 1-800-848-2928 (USA) or 1-800-387-3178 (Canada).
World Almanac® Library's fax: (414) 332-3567.

Library of Congress Cataloging-in-Publication Data

Barber, Nicola.
    Istanbul / by Nicola Barber.
        p. cm. — (Great cities of the world)
    Includes bibliographical references and index.
    ISBN 0-8368-5050-5 (lib. bdg.)
    ISBN 0-8368-5210-9 (softcover)
    1. Istanbul (Turkey)—Juvenile literature. I. Title. II. Series.
    DR719.B357   2005
    949.61'8—dc22   2005042112

First published in 2006 by
World Almanac® Library
A Member of the WRC Media Family of Companies
330 West Olive Street, Suite 100
Milwaukee, WI 53212 USA

Copyright © 2006 by World Almanac® Library.

Produced by Discovery Books
Editors: Valerie Weber and Kathryn Walker
Series designers: Laurie Shock, Keith Williams
Designer and page production: Keith Williams
Photo researcher: Rachel Tisdale
Diagrams: Rob Norridge
Maps: Stefan Chabluk
World Almanac® Library editorial direction: Mark J. Sachner
World Almanac® Library editor: Gini Holland
World Almanac® Library art direction: Tammy West
World Almanac® Library graphic design: Scott M. Krall
World Almanac® Library production: Jessica Morris

Photo credits: AKG-Images: p. 10; AKG-Images/Erich Lessing: p. 12; AKG-Images/Ullstein bild: pp. 13, 14, 22, 30, 36, 43;
Corbis/Lynsey Addario: p. 37; Getty Images/AFP/Gerard Cerles: p. 34; Getty Images/AFP/Mustafa Ozer: pp. 17, 20; Getty
Images/AFP/Janek Skarzynski: p. 38; Getty Images/Ali Kabas: p. 5; Getty Images/Stone/Robert Frerck: p. 19; Getty Images/
R. Winter: pp. 28, 32; Panos Pictures: pp. 7, 16, 18, 31, 39; Still Pictures/Ron Gilling: cover and title page; Still Pictures/
Jochen Tack: p. 26; Still Pictures/Paul van Riel: p. 42; Trip: pp. 8, 40; Trip/A.Ghazzal: p. 24; Trip/Bob Turner: p. 4.

**Cover: Ferries dock at Eminönü along the Golden Horn, an inlet off the Bosporus that divides the European
side of the city.**

Printed in Canada

1 2 3 4 5 6 7 8 9 09 08 07 06 05

Contents

Introduction

Istanbul is unique in the world because part of it is in Europe and the other part is in Asia. The city straddles the southern end of the Strait of Bosporus that connects the Black Sea to the north with the Sea of Marmara to the south.

Istanbul has a long and colorful history; the Roman, Byzantine, and Ottoman empires each claimed the city as its capital in turn. The modern city is a vibrant center of history and culture. Although it is the largest city in Turkey and an important industrial and business center, Istanbul is not the capital of the country: Ankara is. Tourism provides income for many residents. Visitors come from all over the world to marvel at the Ottoman palaces, shop in the Grand Bazaar, and experience the unique atmosphere of this bustling city.

◄ *This is the view from the Galata Tower in Beyoglu on the Golden Horn's eastern side. In the distance stands the new Galata bridge, which crosses the Golden Horn as it opens out into the Bosporus.*

Geography

The Asian side of the city is on the eastern shore of the Bosporus and includes districts such as Kadiköy and Üsküdar. A freshwater estuary known as the Golden Horn flows through the European side of the city. On the western side of the Golden Horn lie the main historic districts: Sultanahmet, home to the Topkapi Palace and the Hagia Sophia Mosque, and the old districts of Fatih, Fener, and Balat. On the eastern side of the Golden Horn lies Beyoglu and Galatasaray, where one of Istanbul's main shopping streets, the Istiklal Caddesi, is located. Four bridges cross the Golden Horn: the Haliç, the old Galata, the new Galata, and the Atatürk. Two bridges span the Bosporus and form part of the highway network around Istanbul.

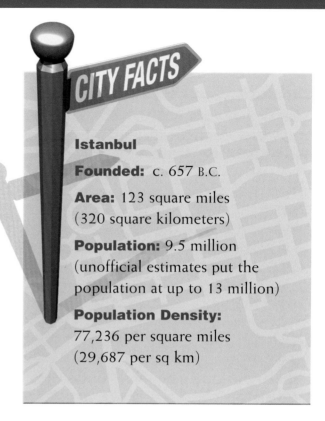

CITY FACTS

Istanbul

Founded: c. 657 B.C.

Area: 123 square miles (320 square kilometers)

Population: 9.5 million (unofficial estimates put the population at up to 13 million)

Population Density: 77,236 per square miles (29,687 per sq km)

Earthquakes

Istanbul and much of northern Turkey lie on top of a large crack in the earth's surface. Known as the North Anatolian Fault, the crack marks the two edges of the African tectonic plate that lies in the south and the Eurasian plate that lies in the north. As the African plate pushes slowly northward, the Eurasian plate moves southward, causing massive instability along the line of the fault. Stresses in the fault build up and are occasionally released in movements known as earthquakes.

Since ancient times, earthquakes have rocked Istanbul. The latest one was in 1999,

◀ *The powerful earthquake that hit western Turkey in 1999 caused buildings to collapse, trapping and killing thousands of people.*

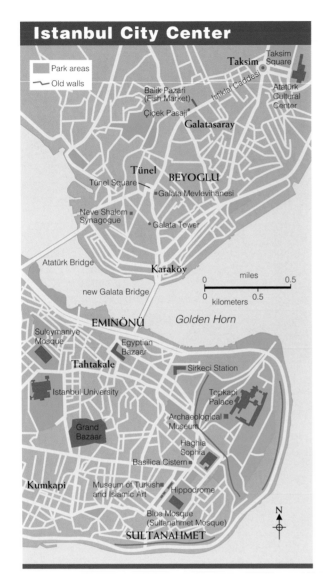

Istanbul City Center

Park areas
Old walls

Taksim
Taksim Square
Balik Pazari (Fish Market)
İstiklal Caddesi
Atatürk Cultural Center
Çiçek Pasaji
Galatasaray
Tünel
BEYOGLU
Tünel Square
Galata Mevlevihanesi
Neve Shalom Synagogue
Galata Tower
Atatürk Bridge
Karaköy
new Galata Bridge
miles   0   0.5
kilometers   0   0.5
EMINÖNÜ
Golden Horn
Süleymaniye Mosque
Egyptian Bazaar
Tahtakale
Sirkeci Station
Istanbul University
Topkapi Palace
Grand Bazaar
Archaeological Museum
Haghia Sophia
Basilica Cistern
Kumkapi
Museum of Turkish and Islamic Art
Hippodrome
Blue Mosque (Sultanahmet Mosque)
SULTANAHMET
N

Istanbul Metropolitan map

Built-up areas
miles   0   5
kilometers   0   5
N
Bosporus
EUROPE
Istinye
Bebek
Golden Horn
Ortaköy
Bosporus Bridge
ASIA
Balat Fener
Beyoglu
Dolmabahçe Palace
Fatih
Eminönü Aksaray
Üsküdar
Atatürk Airport
Zeytinburnu
Kumkapi
Haydarpasa Station
Moda Kadiköy
Sea of Marmara
Princes' Islands
Suadiye

▲ *The area north of the city contains reservoirs and forests that help protect water supplies from pollution.*

when an earthquake centered in the city of Izmit east of Istanbul devastated Avcilar, a suburb of Istanbul. Thousands of people in Turkey were killed, and many thousands more left homeless. Most disturbing, however, is the pattern that has been repeated throughout history: an earthquake shakes the Izmit area and is followed by another one closer to Istanbul. Today, the city's Disaster Coordination Center is preparing for the next "big one."

Istanbul's Climate

During the winter months from November through February or March, Istanbul is cold and often wet. High humidity and bitter winds make the temperature feel much lower than the average 41° Fahrenheit

"The gardens that peep out here and there, the great globes of the mosques, and the countless minarets that meet the eye everywhere . . . Constantinople makes a noble picture."

—Mark Twain in *The Innocents Abroad*, 1869.

Istanbul's Architecture

Istanbul is home to some of the most remarkable buildings in the world. When the sixth-century ruler of Constantinople, Justinian, ordered the Hagia Sophia Church (pictured above) *built, he employed two mathematicians to design the vast dome that covers the interior's wide expanse. Forty ribs resting on pillars concealed in the walls support the dome; it appears to float over the floor below at a height of more than 164 feet (50 meters). Procopius, a Byzantine scholar, described it as "appearing to be suspended from heaven by a golden chain." Centuries later, the Ottoman architect Mimar Sinan, admiring the dome of the Hagia Sophia, determined to outdo it in size. He eventually succeeded in the Selimiye Mosque in Edirne, Turkey. Sinan was also responsible for hundreds of buildings in Istanbul, including the remarkable Süleymaniye Mosque that still dominates the skyline of the city.*

(5° Celsius). Sometimes, when temperatures drop below 32° F (0° C), snow falls and covers the city, usually bringing the whole place to a standstill. Summers are hot, with temperatures averaging 77° F to 86° F (25° C to 30° C) and sometimes going as high as 95° F (35° C). Humidity is lower in the summer months, however, and there is little rain. The spring and autumn seasons are the mildest and most pleasant times of year.

CHAPTER 1

History of Istanbul

Although the historical date of the legendary foundation of a settlement on the site of Istanbul is around 657 B.C., there is evidence that shows people lived there much earlier. Archaeological finds reveal that the area has been inhabited since the Stone Age, as early as 7500 B.C.

Linking the Mediterranean and Black Seas, the Bosporus Strait has provided an important trade route since ancient times. Around 675 B.C., a group of Greeks from the ancient city of Megara founded a settlement called Chalcedon on the Asian side of the present-day city, at Kadiköy. According to legend, another group of colonists from Megara, led by a man called Byzas, set out in the 650s B.C. to look for a place to establish a new settlement. Before leaving Megara, Byzas consulted the oracle at Delphi, who told him to look for a place "opposite the land of the blind." When Byzas sailed up the Bosporus and saw the colony of Chalcedon on the one side and the natural harbor of the Golden Horn on the other, he decided that the people of Chalcedon were "blind" not to have chosen the obviously better site. The settlement came to be called Byzantion after him.

◄ This Byzantine mosaic of Christ is in Haghia Sophia, the church built by Justinian in the sixth century. After the Ottomans conquered the city in 1453, Haghia Sophia was turned into a mosque.

Byzantium

Byzantion became a successful Greek city-state. Because of the importance of its geographic position, however, various regional powers conquered and ruled the city over the following centuries. The Persians, Athenians, Spartans, and Macedonians all laid claim to Byzantion.

In 133 B.C., it became a province of the Roman Empire, and Byzantion was renamed Byzantium in the A.D. 70s when it came under the direct rule of Rome. As part of the Roman Empire, the city enjoyed a peaceful and prosperous time until A.D. 196, when Byzantium supported the losing side in a Roman civil war. The victor, Septimius Severus, besieged the city in revenge, killing many of its inhabitants and destroying most of its buildings. The city was quickly rebuilt on a much grander scale, however, although little now remains of either the early Greek city or this Roman version. Only the outlines of the Hippodrome, a huge stadium built by Septimius Severus, survive.

Constantine

By the end of the third century, the Roman Empire had become too vast to be ruled from Rome, and it was divided into two. This arrangement led to civil war, however, and in A.D. 324, the ruler of the western part, Constantine, defeated Licinius, ruler of the eastern part. Constantine reunited the empire under one ruler. He moved the empire's capital from Rome to Byzantium, enlarging and rebuilding the city. He renamed it Nova Roma, "New Rome," although it soon became known as Constantinople.

Constantine established his new capital as a Christian city. He himself had adopted this young religion in 312 and had declared Christianity to be the official religion of the Roman Empire a year later. To settle disputes within the early Christian Church, Constantine called a church council in 325 at Nicaea (present-day Iznik). It was here that the system of Christian belief known as the Nicene Creed, still used by many Christians today, was drawn up.

Constantine died in 337. During the following years, the Roman Empire began to decline, and barbarians looted Rome itself. Constantinople continued to flourish,

An Enormous Undertaking

People were astonished when Constantine marked out the position of the city walls of his new capital at Byzantium. They were far outside the line of the old walls; many believed that such a vast city would never be built. The city was completed in only six years, however, and in 330, Byzantium became the Christian capital of the Roman Empire. Constantine built a great imperial palace, several forums, and churches. Little remains of his city today, except for one column, known as the Burnt Column because it has survived so many fires. A magnificent statue of Constantine once stood on top of this column, which was erected to celebrate the founding of the new Roman capital.

however, developing into a wealthy and powerful center of commerce and trade. Theodosius (who ruled from 408 to 450) even had to build new walls around the growing city to defend it from the forces of Attila the Hun; these walls still stand.

The Nika Riots

By the middle of the sixth century, Rome had lost most of its control over the lands to the west. When Justinian ruled Constantinople (527-565), the empire was known as the Byzantine Empire and extended to cover much of the Mediterranean region, thanks to the skills of Justinian's talented general, Belisarius. In 532, riots erupted in Constantinople, sparked off by rival groups in the city protesting upcoming executions. Justinian wanted to flee, but his wife Theodora persuaded him to stand up to the rebels. After days of violence that left parts of the city in ruins, Belisarius trapped more than thirty thousand rebels in the Hippodrome and massacred them, bringing an end to the disorder. As part of the rebuilding plan after the riots, Justinian ordered many churches

constructed, including the Hagia Sophia Church, as well as several huge underground water cisterns to provide a water supply for the city.

Iconoclasm

A time of unrest followed the death of Justinian; the Byzantine Empire shrank as the Byzantines lost control of many provinces. Slavs, Avars, Persians, and Muslim Arabs all attacked Constantinople at different times. In 717, the iconoclast Leo III became emperor. Christian iconoclasts believed strictly in the words of the first commandment—people should not worship "graven images." As a result, beautiful decorations were stripped from the city's churches, and many pictures (icons) were destroyed. The age of iconoclasm lasted over one hundred years, until the 840s.

▶ In 1195, a rival removed Byzantine emperor Isaac from his throne; Isaac's son asked the pope for help to restore his father. The pope responded, sending the forces of the Fourth Crusade to lay siege to Constantinople. Here, the crusaders set up camp outside the city in 1203. The crusaders restored Isaac to his throne, but when he could not pay them their promised fee, they returned in 1204 to loot the city.

Empress Zoe

The Byzantine court was a place of great intrigue and corruption, with tales of murder and dirty deals running throughout its history. When Empress Zoe succeeded her father Emperor Constantine VIII in 1028, she also married an aged distant relative, Romanus III Argyrus. Six years later, Romanus drowned mysteriously while bathing, and the very next day Zoe married her new, younger lover. Her new husband joined her on the throne as Michael IV but died on a military campaign in 1041. When one of Zoe's nephews, seeing this as a golden opportunity, tried to overthrow the empress and send her to a convent, Zoe had him blinded and decided to marry again. Her third husband outlived her when she died in 1050.

The Crusades

The late Byzantine Empire reached its heights under Basil II (who reigned from 976 to 1025), a ferociously cruel ruler who expanded the empire once more. His death marked the final decline of Byzantium.

In 1071, Muslim Seljuk Turks defeated the Byzantine army at Manzikert in Anatolia. As the Seljuk Turks took control of Syria and Palestine, Christian Europe launched a series of Crusades across Byzantine lands to regain control of the area where Jesus lived and died. The crusaders pillaged and destroyed as they went, however, and, in 1204, the forces of the Fourth Crusade attacked Constantinople itself. Italian and French soldiers looted the city, sending its art treasures back to the invaders' European homelands.

The Ottomans

Constantinople briefly became a Roman Catholic city until the Byzantines managed to regain control in 1261. The Seljuk Turks were arguing among themselves, reducing their possible threat to Constantinople, but a new power had already emerged. In the late twelfth century, Turkish tribes under their leader Osman settled in Anatolia. These tribes, known as the Ottomans, quickly spread their influence in Anatolia and beyond. During the early fifteenth century, Ottoman forces repeatedly attacked Constantinople. After a lengthy and bloody siege, the Ottomans finally captured the city in 1453.

Mehmet the Conqueror

After the defeat of Constantinople, the Ottoman sultan Mehmet II entered the city in triumph. Called "the Conqueror," Mehmet II quickly set about rebuilding the devastated city, making it the Ottoman capital. The Hagia Sophia Church was immediately converted into a mosque, the city's defenses were repaired and strengthened, the Topkapi Palace was built, and work started on the Grand Bazaar.

Mehmet also encouraged people to come and live in the city, regardless of their race or religion. The Muslim Ottomans were tolerant

"Sultan of Sultans, Sovereign of Sovereigns, Distributor of Crowns, the Shadow of God on Earth, Perfecter of the Perfect Number . . ."

— Süleyman's official title on imperial correspondence.

▲ *Admiring Europeans called Süleyman "the Magnificent." During his long reign, he established a new system of law and commissioned some of the greatest Ottoman buildings.*

in from the newly conquered lands of the empire, funding a time of splendor. The arts flourished, particularly ceramics and calligraphy. Süleyman hired the architect Mimar Sinan to build the Süleymaniye Mosque and many other notable buildings.

The Janissaries

Organized in the early days of the Ottoman Empire, the Janissaries were the sultan's loyal and formidable fighting force. The Janissaries originally consisted of boys recruited from Christian families in the Balkans who were converted to Islam. Highly trained, they were richly rewarded for their work. As time passed, however, the Janissaries became increasingly powerful and often rebelled against the sultan. Istanbul was frequently a battleground as the Janissaries rioted, looted, and set buildings on fire.

When Sultan Selim III (who reigned from 1789 to 1807) tried to introduce reforms, including reorganizing the army, the Janissaries murdered him. His successor Mahmud II finally succeeded in abolishing the Janissaries in 1826; his newly modernized army massacred them, filling the Hippodrome with thousands of bodies.

of other faiths and allowed freedom of worship in the city. As a result, many Jews expelled from Spain and Portugal took refuge and settled here, and Constantinople quickly became a sophisticated, multicultural capital. At some point, the city became known as Istanbul, although the date that this happened and the origins of the name are uncertain.

During the sixteenth century, the Ottoman Empire reached its greatest extent, controlling huge amounts of land under the rule of Süleyman the Magnificent (who reigned from 1520 to 1566). Wealth poured

The "Gilded Cage"

Every Ottoman ruler was a direct descendant of Osman, the founder of the Ottoman Empire. The sultan's eldest son did not always inherit the imperial throne, however; when a sultan, died, the first son to reach Istanbul could claim the throne. To prevent any plotting that might destabilize the Ottoman state, Mehmet II decreed that any brothers of a new sultan should be put to death as well as their sons. After Mehmet III murdered all nineteen of his brothers upon reaching power in 1595, this drastic measure was replaced. From 1622 onward, the eldest son usually succeeded his father. The reigning sultan imprisoned other possible heirs in great luxury in apartments known as the Kafes (gilded cages) in the Topkapi Palace under strict supervision. During years of imprisonment, many lost their minds.

▲ *The Süleymaniye Mosque was built between 1550 and 1557. The largest mosque in Istanbul, it stands on the city's highest hill.*

The Decline of the Ottoman Empire

The Ottoman Empire had begun to decline after it lost Hungary to the Austrians in 1699. In response, Mahmud II introduced reforms, reorganizing the system of government and introducing the first police and fire services in Istanbul. He also ordered men to wear the fez, which became a symbol of national identity, instead of the traditional Ottoman turban. Mahmud's son, Abdülmecid, continued his reforms. The first bridge was built across the Golden Horn in 1845 (the "old" Galata bridge). Galata and Pera became "European" districts of the city, with streets lined with foreign banks, embassies, schools, and grand mansions. Despite these changes, the Ottoman Empire steadily lost territory in wars with Russia and through rebellions in Greece and elsewhere in the Balkans.

In 1876, Sultan Abdülhamid II established a written constitution and set up an elected parliamentary government. However, this parliament met only twice before he suspended it in 1878; it had done little to deal with problems stemming from Russian attacks on Ottoman territory in the Balkans and Caucasus. Abdülhamid II ruled as a virtual dictator for the next thirty years, although he continued the modernizing process, building roads and railways.

Opposition to his rule came from secret organizations, for example the Committee of Union and Progress (CUP), often known as the "Young Turks." In 1908, a rebellion by the Young Turks forced Abdülhamid II to recall parliament. Putting parliament back symbolized the changes that were shaking the empire. The following year, he left the throne.

During the last years of the Ottoman Empire, Sultan Mehmed V (who ruled from 1909 to 1918) was a figurehead; power lay in the hands of the CUP. Turkey continued to lose its territories in the Balkan Wars of 1912 and 1913. During World War I, the Ottomans sided with the Germans. With the 1920 Treaty of Sèvres signed after the war, the Allies carved up what remained of the Ottoman Empire. The British and French controlled Istanbul, putting a puppet sultan, Mehmed VI (who ruled from 1918 to 1922) on the throne.

Mustafa Kemal, an army general who had helped the Ottomans defeat the Allies at Gallipoli in 1915, began to organize

Atatürk, Founder of Modern Turkey (1881–1938)

Mustafa Kemal Atatürk (pictured above) was born in 1881 in Salonica, a city that is now in Greece but was then part of the Ottoman Empire. As a student, his ability in mathematics earned him the name "Kemal" (meaning perfection) from one of his teachers. He graduated from the War Academy in Istanbul in 1905 and quickly became known for his heroism in action. At the same time, he set up a secret society to fight the tyranny of the sultan. In 1915, his reputation was established when he repelled the Allied invaders in the Dardanelles (Gallipoli); a year later, he was promoted to general. Three years later, in defiance of the sultan's orders, Mustafa Kemal led his troops against the Greek invaders in the War of Independence. When the Republic of Turkey was proclaimed in 1923, he was elected president, and he set about modernizing the country. He died after a short illness in 1938.

resistance and collect nationalist forces. When Greece attacked Turkey in 1919, Turkish nationalist forces led by Mustafa Kemal fought back. The resulting Turkish War of Independence, fought against the Greeks, French, and Italians, lasted until 1922. Victorious Mustafa Kemal abolished the sultanate and the Ottoman Empire in 1922, and the Republic of Turkey was established on October 29, 1923.

The New Republic

The Turkish Parliament proclaimed Mustafa Kemal as Atatürk (the "Father Turk") in 1934; as leader of the Republican People's Party (RPP), he became the republic's first president. He introduced reforms, including banning the fez, adopting the Western calendar, requiring primary school education, and abolishing the role of religion in law.

The new government also decided to move the capital from Istanbul to Ankara because that city was more centrally located and less vulnerable to attack from the sea than Istanbul. Istanbul was also associated with the Ottoman dynasty; in reaction against the old regime, many imperial buildings were sacked and looted. The Topkapi Palace and the Hagia Sophia were soon turned into public museums.

"Ne mutlu Türküm diyene."

(Happy is he who calls himself a Turk.)

—Mustafa Kemal, 1927.

Spy Capital

During World War II, Turkey remained neutral, and Istanbul became a hotbed of espionage, as spies and agents from many countries set up headquarters there. It was also a refuge for many Jews who fled the Nazi regime in Germany. A new tax law in the 1940s (repealed in 1944) badly affected the minority residents of Istanbul—mainly Jews, Armenians, and Greeks—however, and forced many to leave the city. Turkey entered the war on the side of the Allies a few weeks before its end in 1945 to ensure its place in the United Nations.

Tensions and Troubles

In 1950, the Democrat Party, the first opposition party to the RPP, came to power. Politics in Turkey became increasingly split between the extreme right and the extreme left, and Istanbul suffered many street riots and terrorist attacks during the 1960s and 1970s. The population skyrocketed as new industry was set up and people flocked into the city from rural areas to work.

After a period of military rule, elections in 1983 brought Turgut Ozal of the Motherland Party to power. Ozal introduced economic reforms that encouraged even more people to relocate to Istanbul. Many moved into the slum settlements that developed around the edges of the city. Istanbul also began to be developed as a tourist center, and during the 1990s, much work was done to restore the city's heritage and history, as well as to improve its infrastructure.

CHAPTER 2

People of Istanbul

A resident of Istanbul is known as an Istanbulu. While official population figures for the city are around 9.5 million, many estimates put the actual population of Istanbul closer to 13 million due to the huge number of immigrants. Historically, the city provided home to a wide range of people, including Greeks, Turks, Kurds, Jews, and Armenians, who lived peaceably side by side under Ottoman rule. During the upheavals of the twentieth century, this peaceable arrangement broke down, but Istanbul remains a multicultural, multifaith city.

The Turks

Most Istanbulus are Muslim Turks. Originally nomadic peoples from central Asia, the Turks were related to the Huns. During the 900s, the Seljuk Turks converted to Islam and began to migrate westward, conquering as they went. By 1080, they had established themselves in Anatolia (modern-day Turkey), although their power waned in the 1100s. The Ottoman Turks conquered Istanbul in 1453. More recently, a huge number of migrants from Anatolia (the Asian or eastern part of Turkey) have moved to

◄ *Children wave Turkish flags beneath a monument to Atatürk that stands in Taksim Square. The crescent and star featured in the Turkish flag were adopted as symbols of the city of Byzantium in pre-Christian times.*

Istanbul; these Anatolian Turks now make up about one-third of the city's population and are also Muslim.

Jews, Greeks, and Armenians

Jews, Armenians, and Greeks are minority groups in modern-day Istanbul. Around twenty-four thousand Jews live in Istanbul. Many are descendants of Jews whom the Catholic rulers of Spain and Portugal drove out in the 1490s when they refused to convert to Christianity. The Ottoman Empire welcomed these Jews, known as Sephardim. Jewish life in the city centered on Galata in Beyoglu on the eastern side of the Golden Horn and Balat on the western side. In these Jewish quarters, some Sephardic Jews still speak the dialect of medieval Spanish, Ladino. Since the founding of Israel in 1948, however, many have emigrated to that Jewish state.

The Kurds

A large Turkish Kurd community lives in Istanbul. The Kurds originally come from Kurdistan, a mountainous region that lies across present-day Turkey, Iraq, Syria, and Iran. Originally they were probably related to the Persians; their language, Kurdish, is very similar to Persian. The majority of Kurds are Sunni Muslims. During the twentieth century, Atatürk tried to control the Kurdish population in Turkey by banning the teaching and public use of Kurdish—restrictions that remained until 2002. Battles between the Kurds and the Turkish government have continued ever since.

The Kurdistan Workers' Party (PKK) has fought for an independent Kurdish homeland in southeastern Turkey. During sixteen years of violence, thousands have died on both sides. In 1999, PKK leader Abdullah Ocalan was arrested and sentenced to death. Ocalan's sentence was later changed to life imprisonment. The picture (above left) shows Kurds in Istanbul holding posters of Ocalan during the celebrations of Nevruz, the Kurdish New Year.

Istanbul was once home to a large Greek community, but when Atatürk's forces fought the Greek invaders during the Turkish War of Independence, many Turkish Greeks fled in the face of violence from their neighbors. During the 1960s, conflict in Cyprus between Greece and Turkey caused many more Turkish Greeks

"Istanbul ... like Cairo or Mexico City, is a city whose expansion is out of control."

—Philip Mansel in *Constantinople, City of the World's Desire*, 1995.

to leave the city. Today, a small Greek community, most of whom are Eastern Orthodox Christians, continues to live in Istanbul, particularly in the Fener district next to Balat.

The Armenians are probably the oldest Christian community in Turkey. They lived in peace with their Muslim and Jewish neighbors under the Ottomans until the late nineteenth century, when Armenian nationalists began to advocate for an independent homeland. During the twentieth century, conflict between the Ottoman state and Armenian nationalists led to thousands of Armenians being persecuted, deported, and killed. Today, the center of Istanbul's Armenian community is south of the city at Kumkapi.

Religion

About 97 percent of all Istanbulus are Muslim. Since the foundation of Turkey in 1923, however, the country has been a secular state. Although Friday is the Muslim holy day, the official day off in Turkey is Sunday, as in Western countries. The city is still marked by its long history as a religious center and churches and synagogues sit alongside the mosques that dominate the skyline.

▲ *People all face the same direction at prayer time in a mosque in Eminönü Istanbul. All Muslims face Mecca, Saudi Arabia, when praying; a niche in the far wall, called the* mihrab, *shows the direction toward the city.*

Islam

Istanbul became a Muslim city in 1453, when the Ottomans from Anatolia took control. The Muslim faith began in Arabia in the seventh century when the prophet Muhammad received revelations (messages) from Allah, or God. These revelations were later collected and written down to form the

Alevis: Muslims with a Mix

In Turkey, a group of people known as Alevis is broadly Shiite Muslim, although their beliefs include elements from many other sources. They pray in Turkish instead of in Arabic like other Muslims, and men and women pray together in simple halls called cemevis *instead of separately.*

Koran (or Qur'an), the Muslim holy book. Islam means "submission to Allah." The Muslims' faith is summed up in the *shahadah* (declaration of faith)—"There is no god but Allah, and Muhammad is his Prophet."

▲ *Islamic mystics called Sufis use a whirling dance to enter a trancelike state and move closer to God. This practice continues at the Galata Mevlevihanesi, the whirling dervish hall, in Beyoglu, Istanbul.*

Most Turkish Muslims belong to the Sunni branch of Islam. Both Sunni and Shiite Muslims follow the teachings of the Koran. Disagreement after the death of Muhammad, however, led to a split that has continued to this day. While Sunnis believe that Muhammad's successor as leader of the Muslims should be the person best able to uphold the customs and traditions (the *sunna*) of Islam, Shiites think that only someone from the same family as Muhammad should succeed the Prophet.

All Muslims have five duties, sometimes known as the Five Pillars of the Islamic faith: belief as stated in the shahadah, prayer five times a day, fasting during the month of Ramadan, giving to charity, and making a pilgrimage to Mecca in Saudi Arabia. In secular Turkey, the practice of Islam is moderate; many people do not keep strictly to the requirements of their religion even though they consider themselves Muslim. For example, drinking alcohol is forbidden in Islamic law, but many Turkish Muslims enjoy alcohol. Most Istanbulu women wear Western clothes, despite the words of the Koran that instruct a woman to cover her head and body outside her home.

Christianity

The Christian Orthodox Church has been an important presence in Istanbul for many centuries. The head of the Greek Orthodox Church, known as the Patriarch, is still based in Istanbul at the Greek Orthodox Patriarchate in Fener. The oldest church in Istanbul to have remained continuously in Greek hands is Kanli Klise, or St. Mary of the Mongols, one of the few churches the Ottomans did not convert into a mosque. The Armenians and Syrians have their own Orthodox churches in the city, and there are also small communities of Roman Catholics and Protestants.

Judaism

The oldest synagogue serving Istanbul's Jewish community is the Ahrida Synagogue, in Balat. Dating from before the Muslim conquest of the city in 1453, it has been in continuous use ever since. The largest synagogue is Neve Shalom in Beyoglu.

Security is tight at all Istanbul synagogues to protect against terrorist attacks. Despite such measures, however, suicide bombers killed twenty-five people and injured hundreds more in 2003 in attacks on Istanbul's Neve Shalom and Beth Israel Synagogues.

Festivals

Despite being a secular state, the main Muslim festivals play an important part in life in Turkey. Islam uses the lunar calendar so the dates of the main festivals change each year. Two of these festivals, Seker Bayrami and Kurban Bayrami, are public holidays. Seker Bayrami (Sugar Festival) is a three-day festival that celebrates the end of the Muslim month of fasting, Ramadan (called Ramazan in Turkey). During Ramadan, Muslims do not eat or drink from sunrise to sunset. Seker Bayrami is a time of celebration; stores and offices are closed and adults give children candy. Families and friends get together; public transportation in Istanbul and beyond is usually very busy. Kurban Bayrami celebrates the story of Abraham and Isaac as told in the Koran. A four-day festival, it is the most important religious festival of the year.

Marked by special services in the city's churches, the main festival in the Orthodox Church is Easter. Many Istanbulus also celebrate New Year with some of the traditions associated with a Western Christmas, including a tree, turkey, and gifts.

Nevruz

One of the most controversial festivals is Nevruz, the Zoroastrian festival of light that marks the beginning of spring. Zoroastrianism is an ancient Persian religion named after the prophet Zoroaster who founded it in the sixth century B.C. Many Turkish Kurds are Zoroastrians; many others are Alevis. For them, Nevruz marks the beginning of the new year. Many different traditions are associated with Nevruz, but lighting a fire to symbolize peace is an important one.

Unfortunately, in recent times, Nevruz was far from peaceful in Turkish cities since the government banned the festival, fearing that it was too closely associated with the Kurdish cause and the PKK. To reduce the tensions surrounding the festival, however, the Turkish government declared it a national holiday. On March 21, 2004, huge crowds celebrated Nevruz in Istanbul's Sultanahmet Square with the lighting of a fire and traditional dances and songs.

Commemorations

Other public holidays honor events in Turkey's history. Republic Day, on October 29, celebrates the founding of the Turkish Republic in 1923; Victory Day, on August 30, commemorates Turkey's defeat of the Greeks in the War of Independence in 1922. On April 23, Independence Day celebrates the meeting of the first Republican

▲ A couple dance in front of a poster of Atatürk, which is surrounded by Turkish flags, at Istanbul's İnönü Stadium on Youth and Sports Day in 2004.

parliament in Ankara; it is also Children's Day, and costumed children usually parade in the Beyoglu district. On May 19, Youth and

Remembering Atatürk

Every November 10, everything in Istanbul and across Turkey stops as people remember the death of Atatürk in 1938. At the time of his death, 9:05 A.M., Turks observe a one-minute silence. People stand in the streets, while traffic stops and the ships in the Bosporus sound their foghorns mournfully. Atatürk died in a room in the Dolmabahçe Palace, overlooking the Bosporus. Today, all the clocks in the palace are stopped at 9:05 in memory of his death.

▲ *Cafes and small food shops line a street in the Eminönü district of Istanbul.*

Sports Day is held in memory of Atatürk's birthday and the start of the War of Independence with sporting events held all around the city. A special day for Istanbul is May 29, the Conquest of Constantinople, which commemorates the events of 1453. Although it is not a public holiday, there are street parades and other festivities in the city.

Food

At the height of its powers, the Ottoman Empire ruled over many different provinces and peoples; cooking traditions from these many different cultures all contributed to the lavish cuisine in the imperial kitchens of the Topkapi Palace. Much of today's cuisine stems from this palace tradition. Turkish cooking relies on fresh ingredients; many Istanbulus still buy their food daily from local markets, corner stores, and supermarkets.

Breakfast, Lunch—and Pastries

For breakfast, many Istanbulus buy a pastry from a street vendor, either a sesame-seed bun or a pastry filled with eggs, cheese, or spicy potatoes. Another popular meal to start the day is fresh bread dipped into soup. However, a full Turkish breakfast includes cheeses, olives, salami, tomatoes, eggs, bread, and jam, all washed down with tea. Lunch is often a soup made from lentils or a meat or vegetable stew served with rice.

Istanbulus munch on delicious sweet pastries anytime, not just after a meal. Pastry shops sell a wide range of mouth-watering Turkish pastries, often made from thin layers of pastry with nuts and honey. Specialties in Istanbul include baklava, profiteroles (a kind of cream puff), and a type of pudding known as *asure*, or "Noah's pudding," made from dried fruits and beans. This traditional pudding gets its name from the fact that it supposedly contains all the ingredients left in the kitchen of the ark after Noah sighted land at Mount Ararat in the Bible myth.

Fast Food and Fresh Fish

Fast food in Istanbul is found in small restaurants, known as *lokanta*, which sell soups and stews that are kept hot in steel containers. Kebab houses (*kebapcis*) are another part of Istanbul life. The kebab is made from grilled lamb, cooked on a revolving spit. Other traditional fast food specialties include the Anatolian *gözleme*, a pancake that can be rolled up with a variety of fillings, and the Kurdish *lahmacun*, a type of pizza. A cold, frothy yogurt drink called *aryan* often accompanies such fast food.

Not surprisingly, fish and seafood are an important part of Istanbul cuisine. Again, freshness and quality are of utmost importance, and many fish restaurants are found near the fish markets, for example, in

Turkish Delight

Lokum (*Turkish delight*) *is a genuine Istanbul treat. Istanbulus can buy it from Haci Bekir, the oldest candy store in Turkey, which is still owned by the descendants of the inventor of this sticky candy. A confectioner who had become dissatisfied with the traditional hard candies created Turkish delight in the eighteenth century. He called his creation* rahat lokum, *the "comfortable morsel," and it quickly became a favorite in the Topkapi Palace. Today, you can buy lokum made with many different fillings, including pistachios, walnuts, and almonds.*

Kumkapi and Galatasaray. The type of fish people buy depends on the season; during the summer months, their choice is restricted because fishing for many species is prohibited to protect stocks.

Meyhanes

Despite its Muslim population, Turkey has always had a relaxed attitude toward drinking alcohol. In Istanbul, local taverns called *meyhanes* sell alcoholic drinks, including *raki* (an aniseed-based alcohol), and are very popular. People go there to drink and to eat delicious morsels called *mezes* (appetizers). The choice of mezes ranges from stuffed vegetables called dolmas to smoked fish, salads to deep-fried pastries, all served on enormous trays from which customers choose a few items at a time. Mezes often make up an entire meal.

CHAPTER 3

Living in Istanbul

Istanbul's population has been rising steadily ever since the 1950s as immigrants from rural areas in Anatolia have flocked to the city, attracted by the prospects of jobs and higher wages. Many of these immigrants have moved into *gecekondu,* which means "set down at night." These illegal and badly built homes have often been erected and inhabited so quickly that it has proved difficult or impossible for the government to tear them down or evict their inhabitants. Most of these buildings lack clean water and sewage disposal and are often unsafe. Over the years, many of these slum areas have expanded so that buildings that were originally one-story high have been built on to make four- or five-story structures packed with rural immigrants.

Most immigrants have little choice about where they can afford to live; population growth in Istanbul has meant that rents in the city are much higher than elsewhere in Turkey. Often settlers from the same areas of Anatolia live close to each other in the city, leading to districts being known by names such as "little Gazientap" or "new Kayseri" after the towns in Anatolia from which the residents originally came.

◄ *These Ottoman houses are in the Kumkapi district of Istanbul. The area was once a busy fishing harbor and is now well known for its fish restaurants.*

The dangers of such slum settlements were highlighted when tragedy struck in the 1999 earthquake. Thousands of people died in Izmit and Adapazari, cities east of Istanbul, but the earthquake also devastated the Istanbul suburb of Avcilar. In the aftermath, it was found that many of the collapsed buildings had been badly built from cheap, poor-quality materials.

Many better-off Istanbulus choose to live in modern high-rise apartment buildings rather than deal with the problems of renovating and maintaining older properties. Others live in wealthy suburbs such as Moda and Suadiye on the Asian side of the Bosporus and Levent on the eastern side of the Golden Horn. Many people also have country homes on the Bosporus. In recent years, Istanbul has realized the importance and worth of its Ottoman heritage, and the government has made great efforts to clean and restore many old buildings, mainly to attract the all-important tourist trade. For example, the luxurious Four Seasons Hotel in Sultanahmet was once a prison, while the Yesil Ev Hotel was an Ottoman mansion.

Stores and Supermarkets

Istanbul boasts a vast array of different types of stores, from the Grand Bazaar to its modern equivalent, the shopping mall. Every neighborhood has its own local grocery store, fish seller, fresh fruit and vegetable store, and dried-fruit store as well as supermarkets such as Carrefour, Gima,

The Topkapi Palace

The Topkapi Palace occupies one of the best sites of all in Istanbul, looking over the Bosporus and the Golden Horn. For nearly four hundred years, it was the home of the Ottoman court and the center of power of the Ottoman Empire. Sultan Mehmet II built the palace between 1459 and 1465, although there were many later additions. When Sultan Abdülmecid moved his court to the European-style Dolmabahçe Palace on the Bosporus in 1853, Topkapi was abandoned. Both palaces contained a harem, a network of rooms inhabited by the women of the court and forbidden to all men except for the sultan and his male relatives.

Makro, and Migros. Weekly markets (*pazars*) are also held on different days in each district. Some of the fanciest shopping areas are Nisantasi and Tesvikiye, while larger stores are found along Istiklal Caddesi in Beyoglu. Many Istanbulus go to the ancient shopping quarter of Tahtakale near the Egyptian Bazaar, where an ancient bathhouse has recently been converted into a modern shopping center.

Markets and Malls

Several big markets attract residents from all over Istanbul as well as visitors to the city. On Tuesdays at Kadiköy and on Wednesdays around the Fatih Mosque, large markets sell clothes, household items, and food. On the weekends, a huge, bustling

Grand Bazaar

For many visitors to Istanbul, a trip to the Grand Bazaar, a maze of interconnected passages, is an unforgettable experience. A center of trade since the Ottomans took power in Istanbul, the Grand Bazaar (pictured above) contains over four thousand stores as well as mosques, a police station, banks, cafes, and restaurants. Bargaining for a good price is a way of life in the bazaar, as well as in many of the smaller shops in Istanbul.

flea market at Ortaköy attracts crowds. The best fish market in Istanbul, the Balik Pazari, is in Beyoglu. Fruit and vegetables are also for sale alongside its amazing array of fresh fish. Another favorite location for fresh food and other goods is the Egyptian Bazaar, also known as the Spice Bazaar. The L-shaped building that houses this exotic bazaar dates from 1660. The tradition of selling all sorts of spices continues today, although many other goods are also available.

The first modern shopping mall, Galleria, opened in Istanbul in 1988. Since then, others have joined it, including Akmerkez, Mayadrom, Carousel, and Metro City. These malls include features such as food courts, movie theaters, and gyms, as well as a wide range of shops and department stores. Among the best-known department stores in the city are Çarsi, Marks & Spencer, Mudo, Vakko, and Beymen. In general, stores open around 9:00 A.M. and stay open until 8:00 P.M. every day except Sunday; malls, however, are open on Sundays. Some smaller shops may shut briefly at Muslim prayer times, particularly on Friday, the Muslim holy day.

Carpets

Istanbul is probably best known to visitors for its carpets. The tradition of carpet weaving dates from early times when the Turkish tribes lived a nomadic life. Carpets were highly prized as portable and beautiful floor coverings and wall hangings. Women wove the carpets with the same traditional colors and symbols used today. Huge numbers of carpet shops speckle Istanbul, many of them based in the Grand Bazaar.

Education

The modern education system in Turkey was established in 1924 when Atatürk closed the religious schools and set up new secular schools. Today, Turkish children start school at the age of six and must attend until they are fourteen. The school year runs from September to May or June.

Preschools and Elementary Schools

For children younger than six, there are preschools, kindergartens, and daycare centers; some are private and others are attached to state elementary schools. In Istanbul and other Turkish cities, such facilities are increasingly popular as more women go out to work and families need childcare.

Elementary school is free and coeducational. Children usually attend elementary school for five years, then move to a middle school for three years. Recently, the government has introduced new programs to improve elementary education,

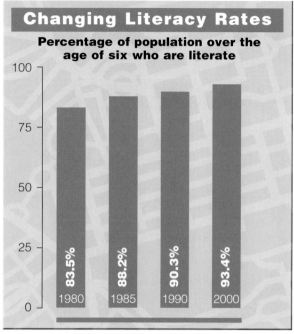

Changing Literacy Rates

Percentage of population over the age of six who are literate

Year	Percentage
1980	83.5%
1985	88.2%
1990	90.3%
2000	93.4%

Source: State Institute of Statistics 2000 Census of Population

▲ *This chart shows how the percentage of Istanbul's population who are literate—those who know how to read and write—has increased in recent years.*

including training more teachers to use computer technology and starting to teach pupils a foreign language in their fourth year. At the end of middle school, pupils are given careful advice and counseling about their options for education after age fourteen.

High School Education

Education for fourteen- to eighteen-year-olds can be divided into two broad groups: general high schools and vocational or technical high schools. In the first group, lycées, or high schools, prepare students for higher education, offering three- or four-year programs. The many different kinds of

"To educate individuals:

- Who adopt the values of the Turkish nation
- Who know the duties and responsibilities to their country and have made them a part of their behavior
- Who can produce knowledge, can utilize the knowledge and technology produced
- Who are democratic citizens and respect human rights"

—The objectives of education according to the Turkish government.

▲ This class in an education center in Fatih is one of many run by the Education Volunteers Foundation of Turkey. This organization offers schoolchildren the chance to improve their knowledge in a wide range of subjects outside the traditional classroom.

lycées include general high schools, science high schools, Anatolian high schools where students study at least one foreign language, fine-arts schools, teacher-training schools, and private schools.

In the second group, students prepare for higher education and learn about industry, business, and the professional world of work. Schools in this group include technical training schools, commerce and tourism schools, and health care, culinary,

Istanbul University

This university traces its origins back to the fifteenth century, when Mehmet the Conqueror took control of Istanbul. He set up religious schools, called madrasahs, *which were later reorganized into institutes of higher education called* darülfünun. *When the Turkish Republic was set up in 1924, madrasahs were abolished, and the Istanbul Darülfünun became the only higher education establishment in Turkey. Renamed the Istanbul University in 1933, it continues to have an excellent reputation throughout Turkey.*

and agricultural schools. Muslim teacher-training schools, called *imam hatip okullari*, emphasize religious subjects.

There are many private schools in Istanbul, many of which teach in English, French, or German, except for lessons that specifically cover Turkish literature and language. The most prestigious of these schools include the Robert College at Arnavutköy, where pupils are taught in English; the Saint-Joseph French High School in Kadiköy; and the German High School in Beyoglu.

Higher Education

Students who wish to go on to higher education in Istanbul have a wide range of universities to choose from. Istanbul University is the oldest university in Turkey, while Istanbul Technical University was established in 1773 and today has highly

regarded engineering and architectural departments. Some universities offer instruction in languages other than Turkish. Classes at Galatasaray University take place in French, while classes at Robert College, the first American college established outside the United States, are taught in English.

Getting to and from Istanbul

Istanbul has its own international airport, Atatürk Airport, which lies about 15 miles (25 kilometers) west of downtown in Yesilköy and is the busiest air hub in Turkey. Another airport, Sabiha Gökçen International Airport, stands in Kurtköy in the Asian part of the city. It opened in 2001 but is virtually unused because it is far from the city center and on the Anatolian, not the European, side of the city. Most flights continue to arrive and depart from Atatürk.

Long-distance train services link Istanbul to cities in Europe and Asia. Trains to and from Europe run from Sirkeci Station near the Topkapi Palace, while trains to and from Asian destinations use Haydarpasa Station on the Asian side of the Bosporus. Many long-distance buses as well as car ferries link Istanbul with places such as Izmir and Trabzon.

Getting around Istanbul

Istanbul's government is investing heavily in the city's public transportation. Every day, the streets of the city become gridlocked as too many vehicles bring the major routes to a stop at rush hours. The network of public transportation includes buses and streetcars; the city is also constructing a subway service. The city government runs most buses, which are red, green, or covered in eye-catching advertisements. Some private buses are orange or light blue.

An old streetcar runs along Istiklal Caddesi in Beyoglu between Tünel and Taksim Square, and a modern streetcar line runs from Zeytinburnu in the direction of the airport to Eminönü on the Golden Horn. The streetcar line links with the as yet uncompleted subway system, which was opened in 2000. On the western side of the Golden Horn, a subway line starts at Aksaray and will eventually continue to Atatürk Airport. On the eastern side of the

The Tünel

Although it has only recently opened a modern subway system, Istanbul can boast the one of the world's oldest underground railway lines. The Tünel is an underground funicular railroad that climbs up the steep hill from Karaköy to Tünel Square at the southern end of Istiklal Caddesi in Beyoglu. Opened in 1875, it is a one-stop, 1,640-foot (500-meter) line. In the early years, horses pulled the railroad coaches up the hill, but today electricity powers the railroad.

▼ *The picturesque streetcar linking Taksim Square and Tünel runs along Istiklal Caddesi in Beyoglu, one of the most elegant shopping streets in Istanbul.*

Golden Horn, the subway links Taksim with residential districts to the north. Work is scheduled to continue on the subway until about 2008.

Not surprisingly, people have a wide range of options for traveling by water—from water taxis and water buses to car ferries and hydrofoils that carry commuters between downtown and the suburbs. During rush hours, travel by water allows Istanbulus to avoid the congestion that builds up on the city's bridges—two over the Bosporus and three (omitting the "old" Galata bridge) over the Golden Horn. Yellow taxis barrel along Istanbul's roads, along with *dolmuses*, which are shared-car or minibus taxis that run along fixed routes and leave whenever they are full. Passengers can ask to be picked up or dropped off wherever they wish along a route rather than having

▲ *Traffic congestion is a major problem in Istanbul, particularly during rush hours.*

to wait for an official stop as they would on a bus. A suburban railroad network also links downtown with the outer districts.

Akbil

Akbil is the "smart ticket" that allows people to use all forms of public transportation in the city without buying lots of different tickets. An Akbil looks like a plastic key with a metal stud and people buy these from bus, subway, and train stations or from Akbil vending booths; they can be recharged at "filling stations" at similar places. The Akbil is valid on most public transportation in the city, including buses, boats, streetcars, and trains, and entitles the holder to discounts of 10 to 25 percent off normal ticket prices.

CHAPTER 4

Istanbul at Work

Istanbul is the main commercial and financial center of Turkey as well as its main seaport. Over one-third of Turkey's manufacturing plants are located in and around the city, mainly in the western and eastern areas. Their main activities include automobile and truck assembly, shipbuilding and ship repairing, cement production, food production, and producing olive oil, silk, glass, cotton, leather, and ceramic goods. Istanbul is an important center for banking and finance, and the Istanbul Stock Exchange was opened in 1986. The commercial center of the city lies on the western side of the Golden Horn, although the new Stock Exchange is at Istinye, north of Istanbul on the Bosporus. Tourism is also a vital source of income for Istanbul.

The Economy in Crisis

The economy of Istanbul and of Turkey as a whole hit a crisis in 2001. Inflation (the measure of how much prices increase) went out of control, reaching 64 percent in 1999. Coupled with the devastating earthquake of 1999 and the corruption scandals that followed, the Turkish currency, the lira, crashed in value in 2001. Hundreds of

◄ *Traders work in the Istanbul Stock Exchange. The Turkish economy is suffering as a result of high inflation and unemployment.*

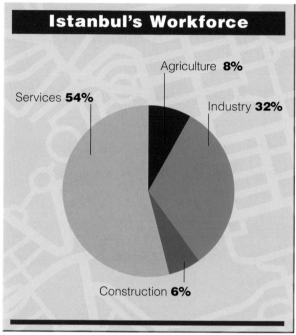

Istanbul's Workforce

- Agriculture **8%**
- Industry **32%**
- Services **54%**
- Construction **6%**

Source: State Institute of Statistics 2000 Census of Population

◀ *In the period 1990—2000 the share of the people employed in Istanbul's agriculture, industry, and construction sectors declined while the share of those employed in the services sector—this includes the retail trade, tourism, restaurants and hotels, transportation, communication, finance, business services, and social services—increased .*

thousands of people lost their jobs in the recession (period of economic decline) that followed. Unemployment hit the poorest inhabitants of Istanbul the hardest and widened the gap between rich and poor.

In response to the crisis, the International Monetary Fund and the World Bank lent Turkey $19 billion in return for reforms in the way the economy was run. The situation began to improve, with inflation down to 26 percent by 2003 and then dropping down to just over 9 percent in 2004.

Running the City

Istanbul's city government is run by the Metropolitan Municipality, which is made up of metropolitan districts, each with its own mayor. Elected for a five-year term, the

Municipal mayor heads the Metropolitan Council. The Metropolitan Council, which also includes the district mayors, is the city's main decision-making body. This council meets typically in March, July, and November, although special sessions can be called if necessary. The Municipal mayor also heads the Metropolitan Executive Committee. Its members include the secretary general of the metropolitan government and the heads of the municipal departments of urban planning and development, public works, finance, legal affairs, personnel, and administration.

The Metropolitan Municipality receives its money from city taxes and directly from the national government. It is responsible for essential services such as providing water, sewer services, and gas and electricity supplies; maintaining roads and operating airports and ferry terminals; providing police and fire services; and planning for the future by drawing up city plans.

The Rise of Islamism

Since the founding of the Turkish Republic in 1923, the country's powerful military has fiercely maintained the distinction between

Recep Tayyip Erdogan

Recep Tayyip Erdogan (pictured above) was born in 1954, the son of a coastguardsman in the city of Rize on the coast of the Black Sea. When Erdogan was thirteen, his father moved the family to Istanbul, hoping to find better opportunities for the children. As the young Erdogan was growing up in the city, he earned cash by selling drinks and buns on the streets. He went to school before taking a degree in management at Marmara University in Istanbul. While he was at the university, he became involved in the Islamist movement, which emphasized Islamic values and traditions.

the secular state and private religious practice. In 1994, the Welfare Party (Refah Partisi) won the municipal elections in Istanbul, and Recep Tayyip Erdogan became mayor. The election created controversy because the Welfare Party was a right-wing, Islamist party, and Erdogan was the first Islamist mayor of Istanbul in a country supposed to be run by a secular government.

As mayor, Erdogan banned alcohol in the city's cafes because the Koran forbids people drinking alcohol. Objecting to making changes based on religion, critics advocated for a secular government. They had to admit, however, that Erdogan made the city a cleaner and greener place. In 1997, he read an Islamic poem at a public meeting and was accused of inciting religious hatred. He was sentenced to ten months in prison, although he served only four months.

The Welfare Party went on to have national success in the elections of 1996. In 1997, however, the military intervened, removing the Welfare Party from power. Accused of breaking Turkey's laws against introducing religion into politics, the Welfare Party was officially disbanded; the government banned it the following year. Its successor, the Virtue Party, was banned in 2001. In 2003, Recep Tayyip Erdogan became prime minister of Turkey after victory in the general election for another, more moderate, Islamist party, the Justice and Development Party (Adalet ve Kalkinma Partisi).

In his new role as prime minister, Erdogan has taken a more moderate line than previously, emphasizing Turkey's links with the European Union and avoiding some of the more controversial issues in Islamic society such as whether or not women should be required to wear headscarves outside their homes.

Earthquakes and Other Problems

The biggest problems faced by Istanbul today are a direct result of its population explosion since the 1980s. Many of the poorest people in the city are housed in

Culture Clashes

The opposing pulls of secular and Islamic values can be seen in many different aspects of life and work in Istanbul. One of the most obvious is the issue of women wearing headscarves. According to the Koran, women should cover themselves when they are outside their own homes. In Istanbul, however, the majority of women wear Western clothes and go bareheaded. In fact, wearing the traditional Muslim headscarves is banned in state buildings such as government offices, the Turkish parliament building, and in some universities and schools. When Atatürk modernized the Turkish state, he rejected wearing headscarves as backward looking. In recent years, however, increasing numbers of Turkish women have chosen to cover their heads; some even wear the burka, *which covers them from head to foot, leaving only their face exposed. Now, some women are choosing to study abroad rather than remove their scarves or burkas to enter a Turkish university. Others wear wigs instead of headscarves inside buildings where scarves are prohibited.*

overcrowded slums that sprawl around the wealthier suburbs of the city. Apart from the social problems created by such unplanned development, many of these buildings would be death traps in the event of another earthquake. The lessons of the earthquake in 1999, which killed more than four hundred people in Istanbul alone, show that

such buildings are vulnerable to even small earth movements. It has been estimated that 65 percent of all the buildings in Istanbul do not comply with regulations to prevent collapse during an earthquake. As long as these regulations are not strictly enforced, contractors will continue to dilute concrete and skimp on materials. They will save themselves money—and endanger their residents.

Drug trafficking is another problem for the city; it is estimated that more than 80 percent of the heroin that finds its way into Europe comes through Istanbul. Authorities think that members of the Kurdish PKK do

▲ An oil tanker makes its way through the Bosporus, while smaller boats cross from one side of the city to the other. Carrying cargoes such as oil through the Bosporus presents a potential environmental hazard.

much of the drug trafficking, using the proceeds to finance their ongoing struggle against the Turkish state.

The Environment

During the 1990s, the city government began to tackle the problems of pollution in the air and waters surrounding Istanbul. Clean-burning natural gas has replaced coal as the main fuel used for winter heating, making a noticeable improvement to air quality. Pollution from car, truck, and bus exhaust, however, remains a problem. Shipping traffic through the Bosporus is also a potential hazard because large oil tankers and other hazardous cargoes moving through the narrow straits increase the possibility of spills that threaten the environment.

Terrorism

In 2003, a wave of terrorist attacks shook Istanbul. Within days, suicide bombers killed approximately sixty people in attacks on two synagogues, the British consulate, and the headquarters of a British bank.

More suicide bombs caused further deaths in the city in 2004. The bombings have been linked to the terrorist organization al-Qaeda, which was responsible for attacks on the World Trade Center in New York and the Pentagon in Washington, D.C., on September 11, 2001. The bombings were seen as a warning to Turkey for its support of the United States and its policies in the Middle East, including its war on Iraq begun in 2003. Groups linked to al-Qaeda claimed that the terrorist bombings were the start of a "wave of operations" across Europe. Other organizations have also claimed responsibility for the atrocities, however, including a Kurdish group calling itself the Kurdistan Freedom Falcons. Aside from the horror of the bombings, the danger of more terrorist attacks is a direct threat to the economy of Istanbul because it reduces the number of tourists who come to the city.

▼ *On November 20, 2003, suicide bombers attacked the British consulate and a branch of HSBC Bank in Istanbul, leaving twenty-seven dead and many injured.*

CHAPTER 5

Istanbul at Play

The artistic center of Turkey, Istanbul boasts a vibrant arts scene and many successful festivals and events throughout the year. Local Turkish artists dominate the pop and rock scene, while the city has its own State Opera and Ballet Company and several symphony orchestras. Most classical music and dance is performed either at the Atatürk Cultural Center in Taksim Square or the Cemal Resit Rey Concert Hall in Harbiye. Held every summer, the International Istanbul Music Festival is the biggest, most prestigious event in the arts calendar, attracting big names in music from all over the world.

Eurovision 2003

◀ *In 2003, Sertab Erener, the Turkish entry to the Eurovision Song Contest, scored a victory with the song "Every Way That I Can." In the Eurovision Song Contest, televised yearly, entrants from European countries compete singing popular songs. Erener's song reflected Turkey's vibrant mix of traditions and cultures by fusing Eastern rhythms with hip-hop. Born in Istanbul, Sertab Erener (pictured here) is one of the most popular singers in Turkey. She caused a stir by performing her entry in English, however, instead of in Turkish. The first time Turkey won the competition, it earned the right for Istanbul to stage Eurovision in 2004.*

Turkish Traditions

The various traditions of Turkish music can be heard in many venues across Istanbul. Suppressed after the founding of the Republic, Turkish classical music—the refined court music of the Ottomans—is now making a comeback, with ensembles such as Bezmara playing on original instruments. Performances of Turkish classical music are given occasionally at venues such as the Cemal Resit Rey Concert Hall. Turkish folk music is often associated with the Alevi population and usually consists of songs accompanied on the *baglama*, a type of long-necked lute. *Fasıl* is more lively music,

▲ *Young Turks are seen here celebrating a birthday in a traditional tavern or meyhane in Cicek Pasaji (Flower Passage) in the Istanbul's Beyoglu district.*

often played live in the meyhanes throughout the city. Sufi music, the sound of the whirling dervishes, can be heard at the Galata Mevlevihanesi in Beyoglu.

Theater, Movies, and Nightlife

Istanbul's theater ranges from State Company productions to plays by local writers performed by the Municipality Theater Company. More than thirty movie theaters are in Istanbul; many are

multiplexes. They show the latest foreign films, usually with Turkish subtitles. An annual International Theater Festival is held every spring in the city as well as an annual Film Festival.

Istanbul's population is largely under the age of twenty-five. With its many nightclubs and bars, the city's nightlife scene reflects these young people's interests. In the summer, rich Istanbulus dance under the stars at exclusive nightclubs along the Bosporus. Local specialties include belly dancing (mainly for the tourist trade) and smoking the *narghile*, a type of water pipe that is experiencing a comeback.

Museums

With its long and colorful history, it is not surprising that Istanbul is home to a vast array of treasures in museums and palaces. Stunning places to visit, the former Ottoman palaces such as the Topkapi and Dolmabahçe are open to the public. The treasury of the Topkapi Palace contains

◄ *The sultan and the ladies of the court gathered for entertainment in the Imperial Hall in the Topkapi Palace harem. The* Valide Sultan, *the sultan's mother, ruled over the harem's four hundred rooms, which housed his family.*

some priceless objects of the Ottoman sultans, including jewel-encrusted daggers and thrones.

Other museums display collections showing different aspects of Ottoman life, including musical instruments, textiles, and calligraphy. Istanbul's Archaeological Museum contains a vast range of exhibits dating from the earliest days of settlement on the city's site. The Museum of Turkish and Islamic Art boasts an extensive collection of Islamic art, including a fine exhibition of beautiful carpets.

Sports and Recreation

Soccer is Istanbulus' biggest sporting passion. The three main teams are Galatasaray, Besiktas, and Fenerbahçe. The Galatasaray team has recently moved from its old home at Ali Sami Yen to the new Olympic stadium in Ikitelli. Its colors are yellow and red. Fenerbahçe's team wears yellow and blue, earning the club its nickname, the "Canaries." Atatürk was a Fenerbahçe supporter, but in recent years, the team has been overshadowed by the success of Galatasaray. Known as the "Black Eagles," Besiktas wear black and white. The team plays at the İnönü Stadium, near the Dolmabahçe Palace.

With teams run by the three soccer clubs, basketball also has a huge following in the city. Wrestling is another popular spectator sport, particularly grease wrestling, in which the opponents cover themselves in olive oil before starting. Horses and riders compete at the Veli Efendi racecourse. Weight training and bodybuilding are popular pastimes for the male population of Istanbul.

The water is too polluted for people to swim in the sea around Istanbul, but Istanbulus can escape from the city to the beach resorts of Kilyos and Sile, both on the Black Sea. They can also go to the Princes' Islands and the Marmara Islands in the Sea of Marmara.

A Traditional Cleansing: The *Hamam*

The hamam, or steam bath, is a Turkish tradition passed down from the Romans and the Byzantines. Islam strongly emphasizes personal cleanliness and hygiene, so in the days when most homes did not have a bathroom, a visit to the hamam was an essential part of everyday life. Originally only for men, both sexes later used hamams, although men and women were strictly separated. Today, many hamams still operate in Istanbul, some catering for Istanbulus, others more interested in the tourist trade. The hamam's center is the steam room where people lie on marble slabs, relaxing in the heat. People often have a massage, then a scrub, before dousing themselves with water.

CHAPTER 6

Looking Forward

Istanbul sees its role for the future as an international city, striding across the division between Europe and Asia, a secular city with an Islamic population. The massive population growth of the last decades, however, has left the city struggling. The municipal government has only recently been able to invest in infrastructure to try to catch up. With its historical heritage and its unique geographical position, however, Istanbul has plenty to offer both its residents and visitors.

Future Plans

Plans for the future include continuing to improve public transportation in the city. The subway is scheduled to be completed by 2008; the government plans to improve sea routes as a means of transportation; and there is a proposal to build a tunnel beneath the Bosporus to connect European and Asian rail links.

Meanwhile, work to preserve the historical heritage of the city is critical. The demands for modernization, however, sometimes clash with the need to preserve the past. The construction of some modern

◀ *In a commercially successful move that also preserved a piece of the city's history, the Four Seasons hotel chain converted the notorious Sultanahmet Prison into a stylish world-class hotel.*

▲ These wooden houses from the Ottoman period stand in the city's Sultanahmet district. Increasingly, people are restoring these elegant buildings.

structures in the city seems to have been undertaken with little thought for the impact on their surroundings. In 2004, the United Nations Education, Scientific and Cultural Organization (UNESCO) announced that it would decide in 2005 whether Istanbul would be placed on the World Heritage list. UNESCO listed several concerns about developments in the city, notably the damage the new subway system could cause to vulnerable archaeological sites and the state of many of the wooden houses that date from the Ottoman period. Istanbul's government has responded to these concerns, but there is still a possibility that UNESCO may place Istanbul on the list of Heritage Sites in Danger. Istanbul would then receive special attention and international assistance.

Despite all its problems, Istanbul's most important role for the future may be to provide an example of a truly multicultural city, one that has demonstrated in its past that it is capable of tolerance. To achieve such tolerance is one of the main challenges that face the people of Istanbul today.

Time Line

c. 657 B.C. A settlement called Byzantion is founded on the site of Istanbul.

133 B.C. Byzantion becomes a province of the Roman Empire.

c. A.D. 70s Byzantion comes under the direct rule of the Roman Empire as Byzantium.

196 In revenge for the city's support for his rival, Pescennius Niger, Septimius Severus destroys much of Byzantium.

324 Constantine makes Byzantium ("Nova Roma") capital of the Roman Empire.

330 The rebuilt "Nova Roma" becomes the seat of the Roman Empire but soon becomes known as Constantinople.

976–1025 Basil II rules Istanbul and expands the Byzantine Empire.

1071 Muslim Seljuk Turks defeat Byzantine army at Manzikert.

1204 Crusaders of the Fourth Crusade attack and loot Constantinople.

1261 Byzantines regain Constantinople.

1453 The siege of Constantinople ends with victory for the Ottomans; city becomes Istanbul.

1520–66 Süleyman the Magnificent reigns.

1826 After a massacre in Istanbul, the Janissaries are abolished.

1908 Young Turks rebel, forcing Abdülhamid II to recall parliament.

1914–18 Turkey sides with Germany in World War I.

1918–22 The last sultan, Mehmed VI, reigns.

1919–22 The Turks fight against the Greeks, French, and Italians in the Turkish War of Independence.

1923 Republic of Turkey is established; Ankara becomes capital of Turkey.

1939–45 Turkey remains neutral through World War II, only entering on the side of the Allies a few weeks before the war's end.

1960s–70s Riots and terrorist attacks shake Istanbul.

1980s Istanbul's population begins to increase dramatically, and *gecekondu* are built.

1994 Recep Tayyip Erdogan becomes mayor.

1999 Izmit earthquake devastates Istanbul suburb of Avcılar.

2001 Sabiha Gökçen International Airport at Kurtköy opens; first subway lines open in Istanbul; Turkish lira crashes in value.

2003 Suicide bombers attack two synagogues, the British consulate, and headquarters of the HSBC Bank in Istanbul; Recep Tayyip Erdogan becomes prime minister of Turkey.

2004 Suicide bombers attack in Istanbul; Eurovision is staged in the city.

Glossary

Allies in World War I, the Allies included Great Britain, France, Russia, Japan, and the United States; in World War II, the main powers known as the Allies were Great Britain, the Soviet Union, China, and the United States.

Anatolia the Asian, or eastern part of Turkey.

Balkans refers to the countries that lie in the Balkan Peninsula in southeastern Europe, including the European part of Turkey.

bazaar a covered market housing many small shops.

calligraphy the art of beautiful handwriting.

ceramics the art of making objects from clay.

cistern a tank for water storage.

city-state an independent state made up of a city and the surrounding area.

constitution the basic laws and principles of a nation that outline the government's powers and the people's rights.

Crusades military expeditions authorized by the Pope (the head of the Christian church) during the eleventh, twelfth, and thirteenth centuries to take over from the Muslims the land where Jesus lived and died.

estuary the mouth of a large river.

fez a red felt hat without a brim and often topped with a tassel.

Gallipoli the narrow peninsula that forms the northern shore of the Dardanelles at the western end of the Sea of Marmara.

infrastructure the system of public works, such as water and roads, in a region.

Islamist describes a movement that emphasizes Islamic values and traditions and wants them reflected in government, laws, and culture. The Turkish constitution requires Turkey to remain a secular state so Islamist parties have been banned.

Kurds people originally from Kurdistan, a mountainous region that lies across present-day Turkey, Iraq, Syria, and Iran.

mosque a place of worship for Muslims.

nationalist describes a person, group, or organization that works for their region's independence.

nomadic describes people who move from place to place.

oracle a person or shrine from which people receive messages from a deity. In ancient Greece, people went to the oracle for divine guidance about the future.

Orthodox describes the eastern branch of the Christian Church, which separated from the western (Catholic) branch in the eleventh century; Orthodox churches recognize the overall authority of the Patriarch of Constantinople.

Ottoman describes members of Turkish tribes who settled in Anatolia in the late twelfth century under their leader, Osman.

secular not religious.

Seljuk Turks nomadic tribes from Central Asia who converted to Islam in the 900s. They migrated westward, conquering as they went, and by 1080 had established themselves in Anatolia.

Shiite Muslims Muslims who believe that religious authority can lie only with direct descendants of the Prophet Muhammad.

sultan ruler of an Islamic country; particularly referring to the rulers of the Ottoman Empire.

Sunni Muslims Muslims who believe that religious authority lies with the person best able to uphold the customs and traditions (the sunna) of Islam.

tectonic relating to the movement of the Earth's crust and its sections, called plates.

United Nations an international organization of nations, founded in 1945 to promote peace, security, and economic development.

Further Information

Books
Alexander, Vimala, Neriman Kemal, and Selina Kuo. *Welcome to Turkey.* Welcome to My Country (series). Gareth Stevens Publishing, 2002.

Barter, James E. *Medieval Constantinople.* Lucent Books, 2003.

Bator, Robert. *Daily Life in Ancient and Modern Istanbul.* Lerner Publishing Group, 2000.

Croutier, Alev Lytle. *Leyla: The Black Tulip.* Girls of Many Lands (series). Pleasant Company Publications, 2003.

Davis, Lucille. *The Ottoman Empire.* Blackbirch Press, 2003.

Ruggiero, Adriane. *The Ottoman Empire.* Cultures of the Past (series). Benchmark Books, 2003.

Web Sites
english.istanbul.gov.tr
The official Web site of the Istanbul government, this site offers a detailed history of the city and images of today's Istanbul and the surrounding area.

www.ataturk.com/life.htm
This Web site presents links to information on Atatürk's life and accomplishments.

www.istanbulcityguide.com
You can search this general Web site about Istanbul and see pictures of Istanbul's past and present.

www.roman-emperors.org/conniei.htm
Learn more about Constantine, the Roman emperor who rebuilt Constantinople, later named Istanbul.

www.turizm.net/cities/istanbul/index.html
See pictures of Istanbul and learn more about the city's fascinating history on this Web site.

Index

Page numbers in **bold** indicate pictures.